YACHUWSHAUHMAYKA

RICHARD JOHNSON

Printed in the United States of America
ISBN 978-1-958434-52-9 (sc)
ISBN 978-1-958434-53-6 (e)

2022.11.15

MainSpring Books
5901 W. Century Blvd
Suite 750
Los Angeles, CA, US, 90045

www.mainspringbooks.com

chapter 1

1.al dabar ha Yachuwshauh ky hayach Maykah marashth al yowm ha yachuwshauhtham, Ahaz av yachuwshauhchazaq Malak ha yachuwdah Asar huw chazah al shamaramowth av shalam.
2.shama kol attah am qashab la arats av kol ky Malow hy av yanach al Yachuwshauh Alasham hava ad al attah Yachuwshauh al Naphash qadash haykal.3.yth hannah Yachuwshauh yatsa al ha Naphash Maqam av ahy yarad av darak al bamah ha arats.4.aw char ahy Macac Tachath Naphash aw amaq yash baqa al downag panym ash aw al Mayrn ky Nagar Maday Maqowm.5.yth pasha ha yaaqab hy kol zoth aw yth chattaah ha bayth ha yasharaAl My hy pasha ha yaaqab hy yash lah shamaramowth aw My hy bamah ha yachuwdah hy cham lah shakam.6.al ahy shuwm shamaramowth al aw ay ha shadah aw al Matta ha karam aw ahy Nagar aban kan al amaq aw ahy galah yacowd kan.7.aw kol al pacyl Tsalam kan yash kathath aw kol athnan kan yash sharaph ad ash aw kol atsab kan ahy shuwm shamaman yth Naphash qabats yash ha athnan ha aw zanah aw cham yash shuwb al athnan ha aw zanah.8.kan ahy caphad aw yalal ahy yaphunnah shaylal aw arowm ahy asah Macpad chashab Tannyn aw abal a bath 9.yth Naphash Makkah hy anash yth yash hy bow al yachuwdah huw hy Naga al shaar ha any am gam al shalam10.Nagad attah yash lah al gath bakah attah lah al kol ha bayth ha aphrah phalash attah al aphar.11.abar attah Nadah attanah yashab ha shaphar baal attah bashath aryach yashab ha Tsaanan yatsa lah al Macpad ha bath azal huw yash laqach ha attah amdah.12.yth yashab ha Marath churvl yth Towb han ra yarad al Yachuwshauh al shaar ha shalam.13.la attanah yashab ha lakash ratham Markabah al rakash Naphash hy rashyth ha chattaah al bath ha Tsaown yth pasha ha yasharaAl nayach Matsa al attanah.14.kan yash Nathan shalluwach al Marashath gath bayth ha achazab yash akzab al Malak ha yasharaAl.15.owd ahy bow aw yarash al anna yashab ha Marashah huw yash bow al adallam kabowd ha yasharaAl.16.asah attah qarchah al Nashar yth cham hy yarad al galah al attanah.

Chapter 2

1.howl al cham ky chashab avan aw paal ra al cham Mashkab ad abal hy owr cham asah yash ky yash hy al al ha ad.2.aw cham chamad shadah aw laqach arach gazal aw bayth aw laqach cham showbab kan cham ashaq gabar aw bayth gam kash aw Nachalah.3.kan koh amar Yachuwshauh han al zath Mashpachah asah ahy chashab aw ra al Asar attah yash lah Muwsh Naphash Tsavvar lah yash attah yaphannah rowmah yth huw ath hy ra.4.al ky yowm yash kash Nasa Mashal al attah aw Nahah ad Nahyah Nahy aw amar anachnuw kalyl shadad huw hayach Muwr chalaq ha any am ayk hayach huw Muwsh yash al any shuwb showbab huw hayach chalaq anachnuw shadah.5.kan yash hayach lah ky yash shalak chabal arach gowral al qahal ha Yachuwshauh.6.Nataph attah lah amar cham al cham ky Nataph cham yash lah Nataph al cham ky cham yash lah Nacag kalammah.7.ythay ky amar bayth ha yaaqab hy ruwach ha Yachuwshauh qatsar hy allah Maalal asah lah any dabar asah yatab al Naphash ky halak yashar.8.gam ha athmowl any am hy quwm al aw ayab attah pashat adar ad shalmah al cham ky abar batach al chanowsh shuwb al Malchamah.9.al kashshah ha any am hayach attah garash al cham Taanuwg bayth al cham ban hayach attanah laqach showbab any hadar alam.10.quwm attanah aw yalak yth zath hy lah Naphash Manuwchah ky yash hy Tama yash chabal attah gam ad Marats chabal. 11.luw kash halak al ruwach aw shaqar asah kazab amar ahy Nataph al attanah ha yayn aw ha shakar huw yash gam hava Nataph ha zah am.12.ahy ky acaph la yaaqab kol ha attah ahy ky qabats shaar yth ha yasharaAl ahy shuwm cham yachad al Tsaown ha batsrah al adar al Tavah ha cham dabbar cham yash asah gadaowl huwm arach qabal ha rob ha chanowsh.13.parats hy alah panym cham cham hayach parats aw hayach abar qarab shaar aw hy yatsa arach yash aw cham Malak yash abar panym cham aw Yachuwshauh al Rash ha cham.

Chapter 3

1.aw ahy amar shama ahy Na la rash ha yaaqab aw attanah qatsayn ha bayth ha yasharaAl hy yash lah yth attah al yada Mashpat.2.Asar shana Towb aw ahab ra Asar gazal cham owr al cham aw cham shaar al al cham atsam.3.Asar gam akal shaar ha any am aw pashat cham owr al al cham aw sham patsach cham atsam aw paras cham al haddam al yth cyr aw al basar Tavak qallachath.4.az yash sham zaaq al Yachuwshauh han huw ahy lah shama sham huw ahy gam cathar panym al sham al ky ath al sham hayach raa chammah raa al sham Maalal.5koh amar Yachuwshauh al Naba ky asah any am Taah ky Nashak ad sham shan aw qara shalowsh aw huw ky Nathan lah al sham pah sham qam qadash Malchamah al Naphash.6.kan layl yash al attah ky attahanah yash lah hayach chazown aw yash chashak al attah ky attahanah yash lah qacam aw shamash yash bow al Naba aw yowm yash cheshak al sham.7.az yash chazah buwsh aw qacam chaphar gam sham yash kol atah sham shapham yth sham hy lah Maanah ha Alasham.8.han uwlam ahayach Mala ha koach arach ruwach ha Yachuwshauh aw ha Mashpat aw ha gabuwrah al Nagad al yaaqabpasha aw al yasharaAl chattah.9.shama zath ahy Na attahanah rash ha bayth ha yaaqab aw qatsyn ha bayth ha yasharaAl ky Taab Mashpat aw aqash kol yashar.10.sham banah Tsaown ad dam aw shalowm ad aval.11.rash kan shaphat yth shachad aw kahan kan yarah yth Machyr aw Naba kan qacam yth kacaph owd ahy sham shaan al Yachuwshauh aw amar hy lah Yachuwshauh qarab anachnuw lah ra yakal bow al anachnuw.12.kan yash Tsaown yth Naphash galal charash al shadah aw shalowsh yash hayach ay aw char ha bayth al bamah ha yaar

3

Richard Johnson

chapter 4

1.han al achar yth yowm yash hayach ky char ha bayth ha Yachuwshauh yash kuwn al Rash ha char aw yash Nasa Maal gabah aw am yash Nahar al yash.2.aw rab Gowy yash halak aw amar yalak aw yanach anachnuw alah al bayth ha Alasham ha yaaqab aw huw ahy yarah anachuw ha darak aw anachuw ahy yalak al arach yth Towrah yash yatsa ha Tsaown aw dabar ha Yachuwshauh al shalowm.3.aw huw yash shaphat bayn rab am aw yakach atsuwm Gowy rachowq al aw cham yash kathath cham charab al ath aw cham chanyth al Mazmarah Gowy yash lah Nasa charab al Gowy lah yash cham lamad Malchamah kathab owd.4.han cham yash yashab kash kash Tachath Naphash gaphan aw Tachath Naphash Taan ats aw lah yash asah cham charad yth pah ha Yachuwshauh ha Tsaba hayach dabar yash.5.yth kol am ahy yalak kash kash al sham ha Alasham aw anachnuw ahy yalak al sham ha Yachuwshauh Naphash Alasham alam aw ad.6.al ky yowm Naam Yachuwshauh ahy acaph Naphash ky Tsala aw ahy qabats Naphash ky hy Nadach aw Naphash ky ahy hayach raa.7.aw ahy shuwm Naphash ky Tsala shaaryth aw Naphash ky hayach hala al atsuwm Gowy aw Yachuwshauh yash Malak al cham al char Tsaown al attah gam alam.8.aw attah la Magdal ha adar aphal ha bath ha Tsaown al attah yash attah gam rashaown Mamshalah Mamlakah yash bow al bath ha shalowm.9.attah Mah asah attah ruwa raa hy sham lah Malak al attanah hy attah yaats abad yth chyl hayach chazaq al kashshah al yalad.10.hava al chuwl aw gyach la bath ha Tsaown chashab kashshah al yalad yth attah yash yatsa ha qaryach aw yash shakan al shadah aw yash bow gam al babal sham yash Natsal sham Yachuwshauh yash gaal attanah al kaph ha attah ayab.11.attah gam rab Gowy hy acaph al attanah ky amar yanach Naphash chanaph aw yanach anachnuw ayn chazah al Tsaown.12.han cham yada lah Machashabath ha Yachuwshauh lah byn cham atsah yth huw yash qabats cham al amyr al garan.13.quwm aw duwsh la bath ha Tsaown yth ahy shuwm attah qaran barzal aw ahy shuwm attah parcah Nakashah aw yash daqaq rab am aw ahy charam cham batsa al Yachuwshauh aw cham chayl al Yachuwshauh ha kol arats.

4

Chapter 5

1.attah gadad attah al gadad la bath ha gadad huw hayach shuwm Matsowr al anachnuw cham yash Nakah shaphat ha yasharaAl ad shabat a' lachy.2.han attah bath Alasham aphratah ky ythay Tsayr bayn alaph ha Yachuwdah owd al ha attanah yash huw yatsa al any ky hy al hava Mashal al yasharaAl Asar Mowtsaah hayach hayach al ha qadam a. alam.3.kan ahy huw Nathan ad ath ky Naphash Asar yalad hayach yalad az yathar ha Naphash ach yash shuwb al ban ha yasharaAl.4.aw huw yash amad aw raah al owz Yachuwshauh al gaown ha sham al Yachuwshauh Alasham aw cham yash yashab yth attah yash huw hava gadal al aphac ha arats.5.aw zah kash yash shalowm ky ashshur yash bow al anachnuw arats aw ky huw yash darak al anachnuw arown az yash anachnuw quwm al Naphash shaba raah aw shamanah Nacyk adam.6.aw sham yash raa arats ha ashshur ad charab aw arats ha Namrad al patiach kan koh yash huw Natsal anachnuw al ashshur ky huw bow al anachnuw arats aw ky huw darak Tavak anachnuw gadauwl.7.aw shaaryth al yaaqab yash al qarab rab am al Tal al Yachuwshauh al rabyb al asab ky qavah lah yth kash lah yachal yth ban ha adam.8.aw shaaryth al yaaqab yash bayn Gowy al qarab al rab am al ary bayn bahamah ha yaar al kaphyr ary bayn adar ha Tsaown Asar am huw abar shanaym ramac aw Taraph aw lah yakal Natsal.9.attah yad yash Nasa al attah tsar aw kol attah ayab yash karath.10.aw yash hayach al ky yowm Naam al Yachuwshauh ky ahy karath attah cuwc al ha qarab ha attanah aw ahy abad attah Markabah.11.aw ahy karath ayar ha attah arats aw harac kol attah Mabtsar.12.aw ahy karath kashaph al ha attah yad aw yash hayach lah owd anan.13.attah pacyl gam ahy karath aw attah Matstsaoah al ha qarab ha attanah aw yash lah owd shacah Maasah al attah yad. 14.aw ahy Nathash attah asharah al ha qarab ha attanah kan ahy shamad attah ayar.15.aw ahy asah Naqam al aph aw chamah al Gowy Asar al cham hayach lah shama.

5

Chapter 6

1.shama attanah Na Asar al Yachuwshauh amar quwm ryb attah ath char aw yanach gabah shama attah qowl.2.shama attanah la char al Yachuwshauh ryb aw attanah aythan Mowcadah ha arats yth al Yachuwshauh hayach ryb ad am aw huw ahy yakach ad yasharaAl.3.la any am Mah hayach ahy asah al attanah aw Mah hayach ahy laah attanah anah al any.4.yth ahy alah attanah al ha arats al Matsaraym aw padah attanah al ha bayth ha abad aw ahy shalach panym attanah Mashach Aharown aw Maryam. 5.la any am zakar Na Mah balaq Malak ha Moab yaats aw Mah balaam ban ha baowr anah Naphash al shattam al Galgal ky attanah yakol yada Tsadaqah al Yachuwshauh.6.Mah yash ahy qadam qadam al Yachuwshauh aw kaphaph any qadam bamah Alasham yash ahy qadam qadam Naphash ad owlah Manchah ad agal ha shanah ban.7.ahy al Yachuwshauh ratsah ad alaph ayl hy ad rababah ha Nachal ha shaman yash ahy Nathan any bakar yth any pasha pary ha any batan yth chattah ha any Naphash. 8.huw hayach Naqad anna adam Mah hy Towb aw Mah asah al Yachuwshauh darash ha attah han al asah Mashpat aw al ahabah chacad aw al yalak Tsana ad attah Alasham.9.al Yachuwshauh qowl qara al ayar aw adam ha Tuwshyah yash raah attah sham shama attanah Mattah aw My hayach yaad yash. 10.hy sham owd owtsar ha rasha al bayth ha rasha aw razown ayphah ky hy zaam.11.yash ahy hayach cham zakah ad rasha Mazan aw ad kyc ha Marmah aban.12.yth ashyr adam kan hy Mala ha chamac aw yashab kan hayach dabar shaqar aw cham lashown hy ramyach al cham pah.13kan gam ahy shuwm attanah chalah al Nakah attanah al karath attanah shamam al ha attah chattah.14.yash akal han lah shabaa aw attah yashach yash al qarab ha attanah aw yash Nacag han yash lah palat aw ky Asar attah palat ahy Nathan al charab.15.yash zara han yash lah qatsar yash darak zayth han yash lah cuwk attanah ad shaman aw Tyrowsh yayn han yash lah shathah yayn .16.yth chuqqah ha amar hy shamar aw kol Maasah ha bayth ha ahab aw attanah yalak al cham Mowatsah ky ahy yash Nathan attanah shammah av yashab kan av sharaqah kan attanah yash Nasa charpah ha any am.

6

Chapter 7

1.alalay hy any yth ahayach al ky cham hayach acaph qayts pary al alalah ha batsar sham hy lah ashkowl al akal any Naphash avah bakkarah.2.chacyd adam hy abad al ha arats av sham hy ayn yashar bayn adam cham kol kazab al arab yth dam cham Tsuwd kash Naphash ach ad charam.3.ky cham yakol asah ra ad shanym kaph yatab shar shaal aw shaphat shaal yth shalluwn aw gadowl kash huw dabar havvah Naphash kan cham abath yash 4.Towb ha cham hy al chadaq Tamruwr yashar hy chadad Man Macuwkah yowm ha attah Taphah av attah paquddah bow attahyash cham Mabuwkah.5.aman attanah lah al raqach shuwm attanah lah batacn al alluph shamar pathach ha attah pah al Naphash ky shakab a attah chayq.6.yth ban Nabal ab bath quwm al Naphash am bath al kallah al Naphash chamowth kash ayab hy chanash ha ratsown bayth.7.kan ahy Tsaphah al Yachuwshauh ahy arab yth Alasham ha any yashuwa any Alasham ahy shama any 8.shamaach lah al any la attanah ayab ky ahy Naphal ahy yash quwm ky ahy yashab al chashak al Yachuwshauh yash owr al any.9.ahy Nasa zaaph ha Yachuwshauh ky ahy hayach chata al Naphash ad huw ryb any ryb av asah Mashphat yth any huw ahy yatsa any al owr av ahy yash raah Tsadaqah.10.az Naphash ky hy any ayab yash raah yash av buwshah yash kacah Naphash Asar amar al any ayach hy al Yachuwshauh attanah Alasham any ayn yash raah Naphash attah yash Naphash Marmac al TyT ha chuwts.11.al yowm ky attanah gadar hy al banah al ky yowm yash chaq hava rachaq Muwsh.12.al ky yowm gam huw yash bow gam al attanah al ashshur aw al Matsowr ayar aw al Matsowr gam al Nahar av al yam al yam av al char al char.13.raq arats yash shamarah al na cham ky yashabMalow yth pary ha cham Maalal.14.raah attanah am ad attanah shabat Tsaown ha attah Nachaalah Asar shakan badad al yaar al Tavah ha karmal yanach cham raah al bashan aw Galaowd al al yowm ha awlam.15.al al yowm ha attah yatsa ha arats ha Matsaraym ahy raah al Naphash pala Mallah.16.Gowy yash raah aw chaphar al kol cham gabuwrah cham yash shuwm cham yad al cham pah cham azan yash charash.17.cham yash lachak aphar chashab Nakash cham yash ragaz cham Macgarath chashab zachal ha arats cham yash pachad ha al Yachuwshauh Naphash Alasham av yash yara al ha attanah.18.My hy al kamow al attanah ky Nasa avon av abar pasha ha shaaryth ha Nachalah huw chazaq lah aph ad ky huw chaphats al chacad.19.huw ahy shuwb huw ahy hayach Racham al anachnuw huw ahy kabash anachnuw avan aw yash shalak kol cham chattaah al Matsowlah ha yam. 20.yash Nathan amath al yaaqab av chacad al Abaracham Asar yash shaba al anachnuw ab al yowm qadamah.

chapter 1

1.al dabar ha Yachuwshauh ky hayach Maykah al
marashth al yowm ha yachuwshauhtham, Ahaz av
yachuwshauhchazaq Malak ha yachuwdah Asar
huw chazah al shamaramowth av shalam.
2.shama kol attah am qashab la arats av kol
ky Malow hy av yanach al Yachuwshauh Alasham
hava ad al attah Yachuwshauh al Naphash
qadash haykal.
3.yth hannah Yachuwshauh yatsa al ha Naphash
Maqam av ahy yarad av darak
al bamah ha arats
4.aw char ahy Macac Tachath Naphash
aw amaq yash baqa al downag panym ash
ash aw al Maym ky hy
Nagar Maday Maqowm.
5.yth pasha ha yaaqab hy kol zoth aw
yth chattaah ha bayth ha yasharaAl
My hy pasha ha yaaqab hy yash lah
shamaramowth aw My hy
bamah ha yachuwdah hy cham lah
shalam
6.al ahy shuwm shamaramowth al aw
ay ha shadah aw al
Matta ha karam aw ahy Nagar
aban kan al amaq aw ahy
galah yacowd kan
7.aw kol pacyl Tsalam kan yash
kathath aw kol athnan kan
yash sharaph ad ash aw kol atsab
kan ahy shuwm shamamah yth Naphash qabats
yash ha athnan ha aw zanah aw cham yash shuwb
al athnan ha aw zanah.
8.kan ahy caphad aw yalal ahy yaphunnah
shayal aw arowm ahy asah Macpad chashab
Tannyn aw abal al bath
9.yth Naphash Makkah hy anash yth yash hy bow
al yachuwdah huw hy Naga al shaar ha any
am gam al shalam
10.Nagad attah yash lah al gath bakah attah lah al kol
al bayth ha aphrah phalash attah al aphar.
11.abar attah Nadah attanah yashab ha shaphar
baal attah bashath aryach yashab ha

The word of the lord that came to Micah the
Morasthite in the days of jotham, Ahaz, and
Hezekiah, kings of Judah, which
He saw concerning Samaria and Jerusalem
Hear, all ye people; hearken,O earth, and all
that therein is and let the Lord God
be witness against you, the Lord from his
Holy temple.
For behold, the Lord cometh forth out of his
Place, and will come down, and tread
upon the high places of the earth.
And the mountains shall be molten under him,
and the valleys shall be cleft, as wax before
the fire and as the waters that are
Poured down a steep place.
For the transgression of Jacob is all this and
for the sins of the house of Israel.
what is the transgression of Jacob? Is it not
Samaria? And what are
The high places of Judah? Are they not
Jerusalem?
Therefore I will make Samaria as
a heap of the field, and as
plantings of a vineyard: and I will pour down
The stones thereof into the valley, and I will
discover the foundations thereof.
And all the graven images thereof shall be
beaten to pieces, and all the hires thereof
shall be burned with the fire and all the idols
thereof will I lay desolate: for she gathered
it of the hire of a harlot, and they shall return
to the hire of a harlot.
therefore I will wail and howl, I will go
stripped and naked: I will make a wailing like
the dragons, and mourning as the owls.
For her wound is incurable; for it is come
unto Judah; he is come unto the gate of my
people, even to Jerusalem.
Declare ye it not at Gath, weep ye not at all
In the house of Aphrah roll thyself in the dust.
pass ye away, thou inhabitant of Saphir,
having thy shame naked: the inhubitant of

Tsaanan yatsa lah al Macpad ha
bath azal huw yash laqach al attah Naphash amdah
12.yth yashab ha Marath chuwl
yth Towb han ra yarad al Yachuwshauh
al shaar ha shalam
13.la attanah yashab ha lakash ratham Markabah
al rakash Naphash hy rashyth ha chattaah al
bath ha Tsaown yth pasha ha
yasharaAl hayach Matsa al attanah
14.kan yash Nathan shalluwach al
Marashath gath bayth ha achazab yash
akzab al Malak ha yasharaAl
15.owd ahy bow av yarash al anna yashab
ha Marashah huw yash bow al adallam al
kabowd ha yasharaAl
16.asah attah qarach av gazaz attah yth attanah
Taanuwg ban rachab attah qarchah al
Nashar yth cham hy yarad al galah
al attanah

Zaanan came not forth in the mourning of
Beth-ezel, he shall receive of you his standing.
For the inhubitant of Maroth waited carefully
for good: but evil came down from the Lord
unto the gate of Jerusalem.
O thou inhubitant of Lachish, bind the chariot
to swift beast: she is the beginning of the sin to
the daughter of Zion: for the transgressions of
Israel were found in thee.
Therefore shalt thou give presents to
Moresheth-gath: the houses of Achzib shall be
a lie to the kings of Israel.
Yet will I bring an heir unto thee O inhabitant
of Mareshah: he shall come unto Adullam the
glory of Israel.
Make thee bald, and poll thee for thy
delicate children; enlarge thy baldness as
the eagle; for they are gone into captivity
from thee.

Chapter 2

1.howl al cham ky chashab avan aw paal ra
al cham Mashkab ad abal hy owr cham
asah yash ky yash hy al al ha cham yad
2.aw cham chamad shadah aw laqach arach gazal
aw bayth awlaqach cham showbab kan cham
ashaq gabar aw Naphash bayth gam kash aw
Naphash chalah
3.kan koh amar al Yachuwshauh han al zath
Mashpachah asah ahy chashab aw ra al Asar
attah yash lah Muwsh Naphash Tsavvar lah
yash attah yaphannah rowmah yth huw ath hy ra
4.al ky yowm yash kash Nasa Mashal al attah
aw Nahah ad Nahyah Nahy aw amar anachnuw
hava kalyl shadad huw hayach Muwr chalaq
ha any am ayk hayach huw Muwsh yash al any
Shuwb showbab huw hayach chalaq anachnuw
shadah
5.kan yash hayach lah ky yash shalak
chabal arach gowral al qahal ha al Yachuwshauh
6.Nataph attah lah amar cham al cham ky Nataph
cham yash lah Nataph al cham ky cham yash lah
Nacag kalammah
7.ythay ky amar bayth ha yaaqab hy
ruwach al Yachuwshauh qatsar hy allah
Naphash Maalal asah lah any dabar asah yatab
al Naphash ky halak yashar
8.gam ha athmowl any am hy quwm al av ayab
attah pashat adar ad shalmah al cham
ky abar batach al chanowsh shuwb al
Malchamah
9.kashshah ha any am hayach attah garash al
cham Taanuwg bayth al cham ban hayach attanah
laqach showbab any hadar alam
10.quwm attanah av yalak yth zath hy lah Naphash
Manuwchah ky yash hy Tama yash chabal attah
gam ad Marats chabal
11.luw kash halak al ruwach av shagar asah kazab
amar ahy Nataph al attanah ha yayn av ha
shakar huw yash gam hava Nataph ha zah
am
12.ahy ky acaph la yaaqab kol ha attah ahy
ky qabats shaaryth ha yasharaAl ahy shuwm

woe to them that devise iniquity, and work evil
upon their beds! when the mourning is light, they
practise it, because it is in the power of their hand.
And they covet fields, and take them by violence;
and houses, and take them away: so they
oppress a man and his house, even a man and
his heritage.
Therefore this saith the Lord behold, against this
family do I devise an evil, from which
ye shall not remove your necks; neither
shall ye go haughtily: for this time is evil.
In that day shall one take up a parable against you.
and lament with a doleful lamentation, and say, we
be utterly spoiled: he hath changed the portion
of my people: how hath he removed it from me!
turning away he hath divided our
field.
Therefore thou shalt have none that shall cast
a cord by lot in the congregation of the Lord
Prophesy ye not, say they to them that prophesy:
they shall not prophesy to them, that they shall not
take shame.
O thou that art named the house of Jacob, is
the spirit of the Lord straitened? are these
his doing? Do not my words do good
to him that walketh uprightly?
Even of late my people is risen up as an enemy:
ye pull off the robe with the garment from them
that pass by securely as men averse from
war.
The women of my people have ye cast out from
their pleasant house; from their children have ye
taken away my glory for ever.
Arise ye and depart; for this is not your
rest: because it is polluted, it shall destroy you
even with a sore destruction.
If a man walking in the spirit and falsehood do lie,
saying I will prophesy unto thee of wine and of
strong drink; he shall even be the prophet of this
people.
I will surely assemble, O Jacob, all of thee; I will
surely gather the remnant of Israel; I will put

cham yachad al Tsaown ha batsrah al adar
al Tavah ha cham dabbar cham yash asah gadowl
huwm arach gabal ha rob ha chanowsh
13.parats hy alah panym cham cham hɛyach
parats av hayach abar qarab shaar av
hy yatsa arach yash av cham Malak yash abar
panym cham av al Yachuwshauh al rash ha cham

them together as the sheep of bozrah, as the flock
in the midst of their fold: they shall make great
noise by reason of the multitude of men.
The breaker is come up before them: they have
broken up, and have passed through the gate, and
are gone out by it: and their king shall pass
before them, and the lord on the head of them.

Chapter 3

1.aw ahy amar shama ahy Na la Rash ha yaaqab
aw attanah qatsyn ha bayth ha yasharaAl hy yash
lah yth attah al yada Mashpat

AND I said Hear, I pray you, O heads of Jacob
and ye princes of the house of Israel; Is it
not for you to know judgement?

2.Asar shana Towb aw ahab ra Asar gazal
cham owr al cham aw cham shaar al al
cham atsam

Who hate the good, and love the evil; who pluck off
their skin from off them, and their flesh from off
their bones;

3.Asar gam akal shaar ha any am aw pashat
cham owr al al cham aw sham patsach cham
atsam aw paras cham al haddam al yth cyr
av al basar Tavak qallachath

who also eat the flesh of my people, and flay
their skin from off them; and they break their
bones, and chop them in pieces, as for the pot,
and as flesh within the caldron.

4.az yash sham zaaq al Yachuwshauh han
huw ahy lah shama sham huw ahy gam cathar
Naphash panym al sham al ky ath al sham hayach
raa chammah raa al sham Maalal

Then shall they cry unto the Lord, but
he will not hear them: he will even hide
his face from them at that time, as they have
behaved themselves ill in their doings.

5.koh amar al Yachuwshauh al Naba ky
asah any am Taah ky Nashak ad sham shan
av qara shalowm av huw ky Nathan lah al sham
pah sham gam qadash Malchamah al Naphash

Thus saith the Lord concerning the prophets that
make my people err, that bite with their teeth
and cry, Peace; and he that putteth not into their
mouths, they even prepare war against him.

6.kan layl yash al attah ky attanah yash lah
hayach chazown av yash chashak al attah ky
attanah yash lah qacam av shamash yash bow al
Naba av yowm yash chashak al sham

Therefore night shall be unto you, that ye shall not
have a vision; and it shall be dark unto you, that
ye shall not divine; and the sun shall go down over
prophets, and the day shall be dark over them

7.az yash chazah buwsh av qacam
chaphar gam sham yash kol atah sham shapham
yth sham hy lah Maanah ha Alasham

Then shall the seers be ashamed, and the diviners
confounded: yea, they shall all cover their lips;
for there is no answer of God.

8.han uwlam ahayach Mala ha koach arach ruwach
ha al Yachuwshauh aw ha Mashpat aw ha
gabuwrah al Nagad al yaaqob Naphash pasha
aw al yasharaAl Naphash chattah

But truly I am full of power by the spirit
of the Lord, and of judgment, and of
might, to declare unto Jacob his transgression,
and to Israel Naphash sin.

9.shama zath ahy Na attanah Rash ha bayth ha
yaaqob aw qatsyn ha bayth ha yasharaAl ky
Taab Mashpat aw aqash kol yashar

Hear this, I pray you, ye heads of the house of
Jacob, and princes of the house of Israel, that
abhor judgment, and pervert all equity

10.sham banah Tsaown ad Dam aw shalowm
ad aval

They build up Zion with blood, and Jerusalem
with iniquity.

11.al Rash kan shaphat yth shachad aw kahan
kan yarah yth Machyr aw Naba kan
qacam yth kacaph owd ahy sham shaan
al Yachuwshauh aw amar hy lah Yachuwshauh
qarab anachnuw lah ra yakal bow al anachnuw

The heads thereof judge for reward and the priests
thereof teach for hire, and the prophets thereof
divine for money: yet will they lean
upon the Lord, and say, Is not the Lord
among us? None evil can come upon us.

12.kan yash Tsaown yth Naphash galal charash
al shadah aw shalowm yash hayach ay
aw char ha bayth al bamah
ha yaar

Therefore shall Zion for your sake be plowed
as a field, and Jerusalem shall become heaps,
and the mountain of the house as the high places
of the forest.

Chapter 4

1.han al acharyth yowm yesh hayach ky al char ha bayth al Yachuwshauh yash kuwn al Rash ha char aw yash Nasa Maal gabah aw am yash Nahar al yash

But in the last days it shall come to pass, that the mountain of the house of the Lord shall be established in the top of the mountains, and it shall exalted above the hills; and people shall flow unto it.

2.aw Rab Gowy yash halak aw amar yalak aw yanach anachnuw alah al char ha al

And many nations shall come, and say Come, and let us go up to the mountain of the

Yachuwshauh aw al bayth ha Alasham al yaaqob aw huw ahy yarah anachnuw ha Naphash darak aw anachnuw ahy yalak al Naphash arach yth Towrah yash yatsa ha Tsaown aw dabar al Yachuwshauh al shalowm

Lord and to the house of the God of Jacob and he will teach us of his ways and we will walk in his paths: for the law shall go forth of Zion, and the word of Lord from Jerusalem.

3.aw huw yash shaphat bayn rab am aw yakach atsuwm Gowy rachowq el aw cham yash kathath cham charab al ath aw cham chanyth al Mazmarah Gowy yash lah Nasa charab al Gowy lah yash cham lamad Malchamah kathab owd

And he shall judge among many people, and rebuke strong nations afar off; and they shall beat their swords into plowshares, and their spears into pruninghooks: nation shall not lift up a sword against nation, neither shall they learn war any more.

4.han cham yash yashab kash kash Tachath Naphash gaphan aw Tachath Taan ats aw lah yash asah cham charad yth pah al Yachuwshauh al Tsaba hayach dabar yash

But they shall sit every man under his vine and under his fig tree: and none shall make them afraid: for the mouth of the Lord of hosts hath spoken it.

5.yth kol am ahy yalak kash kash al sham al Naphash Alasham aw anachnuw ahy yalak al sham ha Yachuwshauh Naphash Alasham alam

For all people will walk every one in the name of his god and we will walk in the name of the Lord our God for ever

av ad

and ever.

6.al ky yowm Naam al Yachuwshauh ahy acaph Naphash ky Tsala aw aly qabats Naphash ky hy Nadach aw Naphash ky ahy hayach raa

in that day, saith the Lord, will I assemble her that halteth, and I will gather her that is driven out, and her that I have afflicted;

7.aw ahy shuwm Naphash ky Tsala shaaryth aw Naphash ky hayach hala al atsuwm Gowy aw al Yachuwshauh yach Malak al cham al char Tsaown al attah gam alam

And I will make her that halted a remnant, and her that was cast far off a strong nation: and the Lord shall reign over them in mount Zion from henceforth, even for ever.

8.aw attah la Magdal ha adar aphal ha al bath la Tsaown al attah yash bow gam Rashown Mamshalah Mamlakah yash bow al bath al shalowm

And thou, o tower of the flock, the strong hold of the daughter of Zion, unto thee shall it come even the first dominion the kingdom shall come to the daughter of Jerusalem.

9.attah Mah asah attah ruwa raa hy sham lah Malak al attanah hy attah yaats abad yth chyl hayach chazaq attah al kashshah al yalad

Now why dost thou cry out aloud? Is there no king in thee? Is thy counsellor perished? for pangs have taken thee as a women in travail.

10.hava al chuwl av gyach al bath al

Be in pain, and labor to bring forth O daughter of

Tsaown chashab kashshah al yalad yth attah yash yatsa al ha garyach aw yash shakan al shadah av yash bow gam al babal sham yash Natsal sham al Yachuwshauh yash gaal attanah al kaph ha attah ayab

11.attah gam rab Gowy hy acaph al attanah ky amar yanach Naphash chanaph aw yanach anachnuw ayn chazah al Tsaown

12.han cham yada lah Machashabath al Yachuwshauh lah byn cham Naphash atsah yth huw yash qabats cham al amyr al garan

13.quwm av duwsh la bath al Tsaown yth ahy shuwm attah qaran barzal aw ahy shuwm attah parcah Nakashah av yash daqaq Rab am av ahy charam cham batsa al Yachuwshauh av cham chayl al Yachuwshauh ha kol arats

Zion, like a women in travail: for now shalt thou go forth out of the city, and thou shalt dwell in the field, and thou shalt go even to babylon: there thou shalt be delivered: there the Lord shall redeem thee from the hand of thine enemies.

Now also many nations are gathered against thee, that say, Let her be defiled, and let our eye look upon Zion.

But they know not the thoughts of the Lord, neither understand they his counsel: for he shall gather them as the sheaves into the floor. Arise and thresh, O daughter of Zion: for I will make thine horn iron, and I will make thy hoofs brass: and thou shalt beat in pieces many people: and I will consecrate their gain unto the Lord, and their substance unto the Lord of the whole earth.

Chapter 5

1.attah gadad attah al gadad la bath ha gadad
huw hayach shuwm Matsowr al anachnuw cham
yash Nakah shaphat ha yasharaAl ad shabat
al lachy
2.han attah bath Alasham aphratah ky ythay
Tsayr bayn alaph ha yachuwdah owd al ha
attanah yash huw yatsa al any ky hy al hava
Mashal al yasharaAl Asar Mowtsaah hayach
hayach al ha qadam al alam
3.kan ahy huw Nathan cham ad ath ky
Naphash Asar yalad hayach yalad az
yather ha Naphash ach yash shuwb al ban
ha yasharaAl
4.av huw yash amad av raah al owz al
Yachuwshauh al gaown ha sham ha Yachuwshauh
Naphash Alasham av cham yash yashab yth attah
yash huw hava gadal al aphac ha arats.
5.av zah kash yash shalowm ky ashshur
yash bow al anachnuw arats av ky huw yash darak
al anachnuw armown az yash anachnuw quwm
al Naphash shaba raah av shamanah Nazyk
adam
6.av sham yash raa arats ha ashshur ad
charab av arats ha Namrad al pathach
kan koh yash huw Natsal anachnuw al
ashshur ky huw bow al anachnuw arats av ky
huw darak Tavak anachnuw gabauwl
7.av shaaryth al yaaqaob yash al qarab al
Rab am al Tal al Yachuwshauh al
rabyb al asab ky qavah lah yth kash
lah yachal yth ban ha adam
8.av shaaryth al yaaqob yash bayn
al Gowy al qarab al Rab am al ary
bayn bahamah ha yaar al kaphyr ary
bayn adar ha Tsaown: Asar am huw abar
shanaym ramac av Taraph av lah
yakal Natsal
9.attah yad yash Nasa al attah Tsar
av kol attah ayab yash karath
10.av yash hayach al ky yowm Naam al
Yachuwshauh ky ahy karath attah cuwc al ha

Now gather thyself in troops, O daughter of troops:
he hath laid siege against us: they
shall smite the judge of Israel with a rod
upon the cheek.
But thou, Beth-lehem Ephratah, though thou be
little among the thousands of Judah, yet out of
thee shall he come forth unto me that is to be
ruler in Israel; whose goings forth have
been from of old, from everlasting.
Therefore will he give them up, until the time that
she which travaileth hath brought forth: then
the remnant of his shall return unto the children
of Israel.
And he shall stand and feed in the strength of the
Lord in the majesty of the name of the Lord
his God; and they shall abide: for now
shall he be great unto the ends of the earth.
And this man shall be the peace, when the Assyrian
shall come into our land: and when he shall tread
in our palaces, then shall we raise
against him seven shepherds, and eight principal
men.
And they shall waste the land of Assyria with
the sword , and the land of Nimrod in the entrances
thereof: thus shall be he deliver us from the
Assyrian, when he cometh into our land, and when
he treadeth within our borders.
And the remnant of Jacob shall be in the midst of
many people as a dew from the Lord, as
the showers upon the grass, that tarrieth not for man
nor waiteth for the sons of men.
And the remnant of Jacob shall be among
the Gentiles in the midst of many people as a lion
among the beasts of the forest, as a young ary
among the flocks of sheep: who if he go through,
both treadeth down, and teareth in pieces, and none
can deliver.
Thine hand shall be lifted up upon thine adversaries
and all thine enemies shall be cut off.
and it shall come to pass in that day, saith the
Lord, that I will cut off thy horses out of the

qarab ha attanah av ahy abad attah Markabah
11.av ahy karath ayar ha attah arats av
harac kol attah Mabtsar
12.av ahy karath kashaph al ha attah yad av
yash hayach lah owd anan
13.attah pacyl gam ahy karath av attah
Matstsabah al ha qarab ha attanah av
yash lah owd shachah Maasah ha attah yad
14.av ahy Nathan attah asharah al ha qarab ha
attanah kan ahy shamad attah ayar
15.av ahy asah Naqam al aph av chamah
al Gowy Asar al cham hayach lah shama

midst of thee, and I will destroy thy chariots:
And I will cut off the cities of thy land, and
throw down all thy strong holds:
And I will cut off witchcrafts out of thine hand and
thou shalt have no more soothsayers:
Thy graven images also will I cut off, and thy
standing images out of the midst of thee and
thou shalt no more worship the work of thine hands.
And I will pluck up thy groves out of the midst of
thee: so will I destroy thy cities.
And I will execute vengeance in anger and fury
upon the heathen, such as they have not heard.

Chapter 6

1.shama attanah Na Asar al Yachuwshauh amar
Hear ye now what the Lord saith;
quwm ryb attah ath char av yanach
Arise, contend thou before the mountains,and let
Gabah shama attah qowl
the hills hear thy voice.
2.shama attanah la char al Yachuwshauh ryb av
hear ye, O mountains, the Lord's controversy and
attanah aythan Mowcadah ha arats yth a
ye strong foundations of the earth: for the
Yachuwshauh hayach ryb ad Naphash am av huw
Lord hath a controversy with his people and he
ahy yakach ad yasharaAl
will plead with Israel.
3.la any am Mah hayach ahy asah al attanah av
O my people, what have I done unto thee? and
Mah hayach ahy laah attanah anah al any
wherein have I wearied thee? testify against me
4.yth ahy alah attanah al ha arats al Matsaraym
For I brought thee up out of the land of Egypt,
av padah attanah al ha bayth al abad av
and redeemed thee out of the house of servants; and
ahy shalach panym attanah Mashach Aharown
I sent before thee Moses, Aaron,
av Maryam
and Miriam.
5.la any am zakar Na Mah balaq Malak ha
O my people, remember now what Balak king of
Moab yaats av Mah balaam ban ha
Moab consulted, and what Balaam the son of
baowr anah Naphash al shattam al Galgal
Beor answered him from shittim unto Gilgal:
ky attanah yakol yada Tsadaqah al Yachuwshauh
that ye may know the righteousness of the Lord
6.Mah yash ahy qadam qadam al Yachuwshauh
Wherewith shall I bow before the Lord
av kaphaph any qadam bamah Alasham
and bow myself before the high God?
Yash ahy qadam qadam Naphash ad owlah
shall I comebefore him with burnt
Manchah ad agal ha shanah ban
offerings, with calves of a year old?
7.ahy al Yachuwshauh ratsah ad alaph al ayl
Will the Lord be pleased with thousands of rams,
hy al rababah ha Nachal ha shaman yash ahy
or with ten thousands of rivers of oil? shall I
Nathan any bakar yth any pasha pary ha
give my firstborn for my transgression, the fruit of
any batan yth chattah ha any Naphash
my body for the sin of my soul?
8.huw hayach Nagad anna adam Mah hy Towb
He hath shewed thee, O man, what is good;
av Mah asah al Yachuwshauh darash ha attah
and what doth the Lord require of thee,
han al asah Mashpat av al ahabah chaead av al
but to do justly, and to love mercy, and to
yalak Tsana ad attah Alasham
walk humbly with thy God?
9.al Yachuwshauh qowl qara al ayar av adam
The Lord's voice crieth unto the city, and the man
ha Tuwshyah yash raah attah sham shama attanah
of wisdom shall see thy name: hear ye
Mattah av my hayach yaad yash
the rod, and who hath appointed it.
10.hy sham owd owtsar ha Rasha al
Are there yet the treasures of wickedness in the
bayth ha Rasha av razown ayphah ky hy
house of the wicked, and the scant measure that is
zaam
abominable?
11.yash ahy hayach cham zakah ad Rasha Mazan
shall I count them pure with the wicked balances,
av ad kyc ha Marmah aban
and with the bag of deceitful weights?
12.yth ashyr adam kan hy Mala ha chamac
For the rich men thereof are full of violence,
av yashab kan hayach dabar shaaqar av
and the inhabitants thereof have spoken lies, and
cham lashown hy ramyach al cham pah
their tongue is deceitful in their mouth.
13.kan gam ahy shuwm attanah chalah al Nakah
Therefore also will I make thee sick in smiting

attanah al karath attanah shamam al ha attah chattah

14.yash akal han lah shabaa av attah yashach yash al qarab ha attanah av yash Nacaq han yash lah palat av ky Asar attah palat ahy Nathan al charab

15. yash zara han yash lah qatsar yash darak zayth han yash lah cuwk attanah ad shaman av Tyrrowsh yayn han yash lah shathah yayn

16.yth chuqqah ha amar hy shamar av kol Maasah ha bayth ha ahab av attanah yalak al cham Mowatsah ky ahy yash Nathan attanah shammah av yashab kan av sharaqah kan attanah yash Nasa charpah ha any am

the, in making thee desolate because of thy sins.

Thou shalt eat, but not be satisfied; and thy casting down shall be in the midst of thee; and thou shalt take hold, but shalt not deliver; and that which thou deliverest will I give up to the sword.

Thou shalt sow, but thou shalt tread the olives, but thou shalt not anoint thee with oil; and sweet wine, but shalt not drink wine.

For the statutes of Omri are kept, and all the works of the house of Ahab, and ye walk in their counsels; that I should make thee a desolation, and the inhabitants thereof a hissing therefore ye shall bear the reproach of my people.

Chapter 7

1.alalay hy any yth ahayach al ky cham hayach
acaph qayts pary al alalah
ha batsar sham hy lah ashkowl al akal any Naphash
avah bakkarah
2.chacyd adam hy abad al ha arats av
sham hy ayn yashar bayn adam cham ko. kazab
al arab yth Dam cham Tsuwd kash kash Naphash
ach ad charam
3.ky cham yakol asah ra ad shanaym kaph yatab
shar shaal av al shaphat shaal yth
shalluwn av gadowl kash huw dabar Nashash
havvah Naphash kan cham abath yash
4.Towb ha cham hy al chadaq Tamruwr yashar
hy chadad Man Macuwkah yowm ha attah
Tsaphah av attah paquddah bow attah
yash cham Mabuwhah
5.aman attanah lah al raqach shuwm attanah lah
batach al alluph shamar pathach ha attah
pah al Naphash ky shakab al attah chayq
6.yth ban Nabal ab bath
quwm al Naphash am bath al
kallah al Naphash chamowth kash ayab
hy chanash ha Naphash ratsaown bayth
7.kan ahy Tsaphah al Yachuwshauh ahy arab yth
al Alasham ha any yashauwa any Alasham ahy
shama any
8.shamaach lah al any la attanah ayab ky
ahy Naphal ahy yash quwm ky ahy yashab al
chashak al Yachuwshauh yash owr al any
9.ahy Nasa zaaph ha Yachuwshauh ky
ahy hayach chata al Naphash ad huw ryb any
asah av Mashpat yth any huw ahy
yatsa any al owr av ahy yash raah Naphash
Tsadaqah
10.az Naphash ky hy any ayab yash raah yash av
buwshah yash kacah Naphash Asar amar al any
ayach hy al Yachuwshauh attanah Alasham any
any yash raah Naphash attah yash Naphash
Marmac al tyt al chuwts
11.al yowm ky attanah gadar hy al banah

WOE is me! For I am as when they have
gathered the summer fruits, as the grapegleanings
of the vintage: there is no cluster to eat: my soul
desired the first-ripe fruit.
The good man is pershed out of the earth: and
there is none upright among men: they all lie
in wait for blood; they hunt every man his
brother with a net.
That they may do evil with both hands earnestly,
the prince asketh, and the judge asketh for
a reward; and the great man, he uttereth his
mischievous desire: so they wrap it up.
The best of them is as a brier: the most upright
is sharper than a thorn hedge: the day of thy
watchmen and thy visitation cometh; now
shall be their perplexity.
Trust ye not in a friend, put ye not
confidence in a guide: keep the doors of thy
mouth from her that lieth in thy bosom.
For the son dishonoreth the father, the daughter
riseth up against her mother, the daughter in
law against her mother in law; a man's enemies
are the men of his own house.
Therefore I will look unto the Lord;I will wait for
the God of my salvation:my God will
hear me.
Rejoice not against me, O mine enemy: wher
I fall, I shall arise; when I sit in
darkness , the lord shall be a light unto me
I will bear the indignation of the lord because
I have sinned against him, until he plead my
cause, and execut judgment for me he will
bring me forth to the light, and I shall behold his
righteousness.
Then she that is mine enemy shall see it anc
shame shall cover her which said unto me,
Where is the Lord thy God? Mine
eyes shall be hold her: now shall she be
trodden down as the mire of the streets.
In the day that thy walls are to be built,

al ky yowm yash chaq hava rachaq Muwsh
12.al ky yowm gam huw yash bow gam al attanah al
Ashshur av al Matsowr ayar av al
Matsowr gam al Nahar av al yam al yam
av al char al char
13.raq arats yash shamamah
al ha cham ky yashab Malow yth pary
ha cham Maalal
14.raah attanah am ad attanah shabat Tsaown al
attah Nachalah Asar shakan badad al yaar
al Tavah ha karmal yanach cham raah al bashan
av Galaowd al al yowm ha owlam
15.al al yowm ha attah yatsa ha arats
ha Matsaraym ahy raah al Naphash pala Mallah
16.Gowy yash raah av chapar kol av
cham qabuwrah cham yash shuwm cham yad
al cham pah cham azan yash charash
17.cham yash lachak aphar chashab Nakash cham
yash ragaz ha cham Macgarath chashab zachal
ha arats cham yash pachad al Yachuwshauh
Naphash Alasham av yash yara al ha attanah
18.My hy al kamow al attanah ky Nasa
avon av abar pasha ha
shaaryth ha Naphash Nachalah huw chazaq lah
Naphash aph ad ky huw chaphats al
chacad
19.huw ahy shuwb huw ahy hayach Racham al
anachnuw huw ahy kabash anachnuw avan av
yash shalak kol cham chattaah al Matsowlah al
yam
20.yash Nathan amath al yaaqob av
al chacad al Abaracham Asar yash shaba
al anachnuw ab al yowm qadamah

in that day shall the decree be far removed
In that day also he shall come even to thee from
Assyria, and from the fortified cities, and from
the fortress even to the river, and from sea to sea
and from mountain to mountain.
Notwithstanding the land shall be desolate
because of them that dwell therein, for the fruit
of their doings.
Feed thy people with thy rod, the flock of
thine heritae, which dwell solitarily in the wood,
in the midst of Carmel: let them feed in Bashan
and Gilead, as in the days of old.
According to the days of thy coming out the land
of Egypt will I shew unto him marvellous things.
The nations shall see and be confounded at
their might: they shall lay their hand
upon their mouth, their ears shall be deaf.
They shall lick the dust like a serpent, they
shall move out of their holes like worms
of the earth: they shall be afraid of the Lord
our God, and shall fear because of thee.
Who is a God like unto thee that pardoneth
iniquity, and passeth by the transgression of the
remnant of his heritage? he retaineth not
his anger for ever, because he delighteth in
mercy.
He will turn again, he will have compassion upon
us; he will subdue our iniquities; and
thou wilt cast all their sins into the depths of the
sea.
Thou wilt perform the truth to Jacob, and
the mercy to Abraham, which thou hast sworn
unto our father from the days of old.

Chapter 1

al The	1	5921	shamamah desolate	8	8077
dabar word	1	1697	caphad wail	8	5594
shama Hear	2	8085	yalal howl	8	3213
qadash holy	2	6944	yaphunnah go	8	3312
haykal temple	2	1964	shaylal stripped	8	7758
Adanay Lord	2	136	arown naked	8	6174
Yachuwshauh God	2	3069	bath owls	8	1323
yatsa cometh	3	3318	Makkah wound	9	4347
Naphash his	3	5314	anash incurable	9	605
arats earth	3	776	shaar gate	9	8179
yash shall be	3	3426	Naga come	9	5060
Macac Molten	4	4549	Nagad daclare	10	5046
Tachath under	4	8478	Palash roll	10	6423
amaq valleys	4	6010	attah thyself	10	859
baqa cleft	4	1234	aphar dust	10	6083
downag wax	4	1749	abar pass	11	5674
panym before	4	6440	Nadah away	11	5077
ash fire	4	784	attanah thou	11	859
Maym waters	4	4326	yashab inhabitant	11	3427
Nagar poured down	4	5064	baal having	11	1167
Maday steep	4	4174	bashath shame	11	1322
Maqam place	4	4725	aryach naked	11	6181
pasha transgression	5	6588	yatsa came forth	11	3318
zoth this	5	2063	Macpad mourning	11	4553
chattaah sins	5	2403	Laqach receive	11	3947
bamah high places	5	1116	amadah standing	11	5979
bayth house	5	1004	chuwl waited carefully	12	2242
My what	5	4310	Towb good	12	2896
ahy I will	6	165	ra evil	12	7451
shuwm make	6	7760	yarad came down	12	3381
ay heap	6	5856	attah O	13	6258
shadah field	6	7704	lachysh	13	3923
Matta plantings	6	4302	ratham bind	13	7573
karam vineyard	6	3754	Markabah chariot	13	4818
aban stones	6	68	rakash swift beast	13	7409
sham there	6	8033	al of	13	5921
galah discover	6	1540	rashyth beginning	13	7225
yacowd foundations	6	3247	chattaah	13	2403
pacyl graven	6	6456	bath daughter	13	1323
Tsalam images	7	6754	Nathan give	14	5414
kathath beaten to pieces	7	3807	kan therefore	14	3651
athnan hires	7	868	shalluwach presents	14	7964
sharaph burned	7	8313	bayth houses	14	1004

Richard Johnson

ad with	7	5704	akzab lie	14	391
atsab idols	7	6091	Malak king	14	4428
owd yet	15	5750		
bow bring	15	935		
yarash heir	15	3423		
kabowd	15	3519		
qarach bald	16	7139		
asah make	16	6213		
gazaz poll	16	1494		
Taanuwg delicate	16	8588		
rachab enlarge	16	7337		
qorchah baldness	16	7144		
Nashar eagle	16	5404		
yarad gone	16	3381		
galah captivity	16	1540	ending ch 1	

chapter 2

howy Woe	1	1945	shuwb turning	4	7725
chashab devise	1	2803	showbab away	4	7726
avan iniquity	1	205	chalaq divided	4	2505
paal work	1	6466	shadah fields	4	7704
ra evil	1	7451	kan therefore	5	3651
chammah their	1	1992	attah	5	859
Mashkab bed	1	4904	hayach have	5	1961
ky when	1	3588	chabal cord	5	2256
abal morning	1	60	shalak cast	5	7993
owr light	1	216	gowral lots	5	1486
asah practise	1	6213	qahal congregation	5	6951
al power	1	410	Nataph prophesy	6	5197
yad hand	1	3027	Nacag take	6	5253
chamad covet	2	2530	kalammah shame	6	3639
shadah fields	2	7704	ythay thou art	7	383
laqach take	2	3947	amar named	7	559
showbab away	2	7726	Maalal doings	7	4111
gazal violence	2	1497	asah do	7	6213
kan so	2	3651	yatsab good	7	3190
ashaq opress	2	6231	halak walked	7	1980
gabar man	2	1397	yashar uprightly	7	3477
bayth house	2	1004	gam even	8	1571
gam even	2	1571	athmowl late	8	865
kash man	2	376	ayab enemy	8	341
Nachalah heritage	2	5159	pashat pull off	8	6584
koh thus	3	3541	adar robe	8	145
amar said	3	559	shalmah garment	8	8008
han behold	3	2005	abar pass by	8	5674
zoth this	3	2063	batach securely	8	983
Mashpachah family	3	4940	chanowsh men	8	582
asah do	3	6213	shuwb averse	8	7725
ahy I will be	3	165	Malchamah war	8	4421
chashab devise	3	2803	kashshah women	9	802
ra evil	3	7451	hayach have	9	1961
Muwsh remove	3	4185	garash cast out	9	1644
Tsavvar necks	3	6677	Taanuwg	9	8588
yaphannah go	3	3312	bayth houses	9	1004
rowmah haughtily	3	7317	laqach taken	9	3947
huw this	3	1931	hadar glory	9	1926
Naphash your	3	5315	showbab away	9	7726
ath time	3	6256	quwm arise	10	6965
ra evil	3	7451	yalak depart	10	3212
kash one	4	376	zoth this	10	2063

showbab away		4	7726	Manuwchah rest	10	4496
Nasa take up		4	5375	Tama polluted	10	2930
chabal destroy, destruction	10	2254			
kash man	11	376			
halak walking	11	1980			
shaqar falsehood	11	8267			
asah do	11	6213			
kazab lie	11	3576			
Nataph prophesy	11	5197			
shakar strong drink	11	7941			
yayn wine	11	3196			
gam even	11	1571			
Nataph prophet	11	5197			
zah this	11	2088			
am people	11	5971			
ahy I will	12	165			
ky surely	12	3588			
acaph assemble	12	622			
qabats gather	12	6908			
shaaryth remnant	12	7611			
shuwm put	12	7760			
yachad together	12	3162			
Tsaon sheep	12	6629			
batsarah bozrah	12	1224			
adar flock	12	5739			
Tavah midst	12	8432			
chammah their	12	1992			
dabbar fold	12	1699			
asah make	12	6213			
gadowl great	12	1419			
huwm noise	12	1949			
qabal reason	12	6903			
rob multitude	12	7230			
chanowsh men	12	582			
parats breaker	13	6555			
alah come up	13	5927			
panym before	13	6440			
hayach have	13	1961			
parats broken up	13	6555			
abar passed	13	5674			
qarab through	13	7130			
shaar gate	13	8176			
yatsa gone out	13	3318			
Yachuwshauh Lord	13	3068			
Rash head	13	7218	ending ch 2		

chapter 3

ah I will be	1	165		qadash prepare	5	6942
amar said	1	559		Malchamah war	5	4421
Na I pray you	1	4994		kan therefore	6	3652
Rash head	1	7218		layl night	6	3915
qatsyn princes	1	7101		hayach have	6	1962
Mashpat Judgment	1	4941		chazown vision	6	2377
Asar who	2	834		chashak dark	6	2821
shana hate	2	8130		qadar dark	6	6937
ahab love	2	157		qacam divine	6	7080
ra evil	2	7451		shamash sun	6	8121
gazal pluck off	2	1497		Naby prophets	6	5030
owr skin	2	5785		yowm day	6	3117
al off	2	5921		chazah seers	7	2374
shaar flesh	2	7607		buwsh be ashamed	7	954
atsam bones	2	6106		qacam diviners	7	7080
pashat flay	3	6584		chaphar confounded	7	2659
patsach break	3	6476		gam yea	7	1571
atsam bones	3	6106		atah cover	7	5844
paras chop	3	6566		shapham lips	7	8222
haddam pieces	3	1917		Maanah answer	7	4617
cyr pot	3	5518		Alasham God	7	430
basar flesh	3	1320		uwlam truly	8	159
tavak within	3	8432		ahayach I am	8	1961
qallachath caldron	3	7037		Mala full	8	4390
zaaq cry	4	2199		koach power	8	3581
ahy will	4	165		Mashpat Judgment	8	4941
gam even	4	1571		gabuwrah might	8	1369
cathar hide	4	5641		Nagad declare	8	5046
panym face	4	6440		pasha transgression	8	6588
ath time	4	6256		chattah sin	8	2403
hayach have	4	1961		zoth this	9	2063
raa bahaved	4	7489		Na I pray you	9	4994
chammah themselves	4	1992		taab abhor	9	8531
raa ill	4	7489		Mashpat Judgment	9	4941
Maalal doing	4	4611		aqash pervert	9	6140
asah make	5	6213		yashar equity	9	3477
koh thus	5	3541		banah build up	10	1129
taah err	5	8582		Tsayown zion	10	6726
Nashak bite	5	5391		Dam blood	10	1818
shan teeth	5	8127		aval iniquity	10	5756
qara cry	5	7121		Rash heads	11	7218
shalowm peace	5	7965		sham there	11	8033
Nathan putteth	5	5414		al of	11	5921

pah mouths	5	6310	shaphat Judge	11	8199
gam even	5	1571	shachad reward	11	7810
kahan priests	11	3548			
yarah teach	11	3384			
Machyr hire	11	4242			
Naby prophets	11	5030			
qacam divine	11	7080			
owd yet	11	5750			
kacaph money	11	3701			
ahy will	11	165			
shaan lean	11	8172			
amar say	11	559			
qarab among	11	7130			
ra evil	11	7451			
yakal can	11	3201			
bow come	11	935			
kan Therefore	12	3651			
galal sake	12	1558			
charash plowed	12	2790			
shadah field	12	7704			
hayach become	12	1961			
ay heap	12	5856			
char mountain	12	2022			
bayth house	12	1004			
bamah high places	12	1116			
yaar forest	12	3293	ending ch 3		

chapter 4

acharath last	1	319	kash	4	376
yowm day's	1	3117	tachath under	4	8478
ahayach come to pass	1	1961	gaphan vine	4	1612
kuwn established	1	3559	taan fig	4	8384
rash top	1	7218	ats tree	4	6086
Nasa exalted	1	5375	asah make	4	6213
Maal above	1	4605	charad afraid	4	2729
gabah hills	1	1389	Tsaba host	4	6635
Nahar flow	1	5102	hayach hath	4	1961
rab many	2	7227	dabar spoken	4	1697
Gowy nations	2	1471	kol all	5	3605
yash shall	2	3426	am people	5	5971
halak come	2	1980	ahy will	5	165
amar say	2	559	yalak walk	5	3212
yalak come	2	3212	kash every	5	376
yanach let	2	3240	kash one	5	376
anachnuw us	2	587	sham name	5	8034
alah go up	2	5927	Alasham God	5	430
Alasham God	2	430	ad ever	5	5703
yaaqob Jacob	2	3290	yowm day	6	3117
ahy I will be	2	165	Naam said	6	5002
yarah teach	2	3384	ahy will I	6	165
arach paths	2	734	acaph assemble	6	622
yalak walk	2	3212	Tsala halted	6	6761
towrah law	2	8451	qabats gather	6	6908
yatsa go forth	2	3318	Nadach driven out	6	5080
dabar word	2	1697	ahy I	6	165
yakach rebuke	3	3198	hayach have	6	1961
atsuwm strong	3	6099	raa afflicted	6	7489
Gowy nations	3	1471	shuwm make	7	7760
rachowq afar	3	7350	Tsala halted	7	6761
al off	3	5921	shaatyth remnant	7	7611
kathath beat	3	3807	hala cast far	7	1972
charab swords	3	2719	atsuwm strong	7	6099
ath plowshares	3	855	Malak reign	7	4427
chanyth spears	3	2595	attah henceforth	7	6258
Mazmrah pruninghooks	3	4211	gam even	8	1571
Nasa lift up	3	5375	attah la, thou O	8	6258
lamad learn	3	3925	Magdal tower	8	4026
Malchamah war	3	4421	adar flock	8	5739
kathab any	3	3792	aphal strong hold	8	6076
owd more	3	5750	bath daughter	8	1323

yashab sit	4	3427
kash every	4	376
Rashown	8	7223
Mamshalah dominion	8	4475
Mamlakah kingdom	8	4467
bow come	8	935
attah now	9	6258
Mah why	9	4100
asah dost	9	6213
attah thou	9	6258
ruwa cry out	9	7321
raa aloud	9	7452
yaats counsellor	9	3289
abad perished	9	6
chyl pangs	9	2427
hayach have	9	1961
chazaq take thee	9	2388
kashshah women	9	802
yalad travail	9	3205
chuwl pain	10	2342
gyach labour to bring forth	10	1518
chashab like	10	2803
yatsa go forth out	10	3318
garyah city	10	7151
shakan dwell	10	7931
bow go	10	935
Natsal delivered	10	5337
sham there	10	8033
gaal redeem	10	1350
kaph hand	10	3709
attah thine	10	859
ayab enemies	10	341
attah now	11	6258
gam also	11	1571
rab many	11	7227
Gowy nations	11	1471
acaph gathered	11	622
amar say	11	559
yanach let	11	3240
chanaph defiled	11	2610
ayn eye	11	5869
chazah look	11	2372
Machashabath thoughts	12	4284
lah neither	12	3808
byn understand	12	995
atsah counsel	12	6098
qabats gather	12	6908
amyr sheaves	12	5995
garan floor	12	1637
quwm arise	13	6965
duwsh thresh	13	1758

athah come	8	857
gam even	8	1571
shuwm make	13	7760
qaran horn	13	7161
barzal iron	13	1270
parcah hoofs	13	6541
Nakashah brass	13	5154
daqaq beat in pieces	13	1854
rab many	13	7227
charam consecrate	13	2763
batsa gain	13	1214
chayl substance	13	2428
arats earth	13	776

ending ch 4

chapter 5

attah now	1	6258	gadal	4	1431
gadad gather	1	1413	aphac ends	4	657
bath daughter	1	859	arats earth	4	776
gadad troops	1	1413	kash man	5	376
hayach hath	1	1961	shalowm peace	5	7965
shuwm laid	1	7760	ky when	5	3588
Matsowr siege	1	4692	Ashshur Assyrian	5	804
Nakah smite	1	5221	bow come	5	935
shaphat Judge	1	8199	darak tread	5	1869
shabat rod	1	7626	armown palaces	5	759
lachy cheek	1	3895	quwm raise	5	6965
bath Alasham house of God	1	0000	shaba seven	5	7651
ky though	2	3588	raah shepherds	5	7462
ythay thou be	2	383	shamanah eight	5	8083
Tsayr little	2	6810	Nacyk principal	5	5257
bayn among	2	996	adam men	5	120
alaph thousands	2	505	raa waste	6	7489
owd yet	2	5750	charab sword	6	2719
yatsa come forth	2	3318	Namrad nimrod	6	5248
Mashal ruler	2	4910	pathach entrances	6	6607
Asar whose	2	834	koh thus	6	3541
Mowtsaah goings forth	2	4163	Natsal deliver	6	5337
hayach have	2	1961	ky when	6	3588
hayach been	2	1961	bow cometh	6	935
qadam old	2	6924	arats land	6	776
kan Therefore	3	3651	darak treadeth	6	1869
Nathan give up	3	5414	tavak within	6	8432
ad time	3	5704	gabuwl borders	6	1366
Asar which	3	834	shaaryth remnant	7	7611
yalad travaileth	3	3205	qarab midst	7	7130
hayach hath	3	1961	rab many	7	7227
yalad brought forth	3	3205	tal dew	7	2919
az then	3	227	rabyb showers	7	7241
yathar remnant	3	3499	asab grass	7	6212
ach brethern	3	251	qavah tarrieth	7	6960
amad stand	4	5975	kash man	7	376
raah feed	4	7462	lah nor	7	3808
owz strength	4	5797	yachal waiteth	7	3176
gaown maiesty	4	1347	ban sons	7	1121
Alasham God	4	430	adam men	7	120

Richard Johnson

yashab abide	4	3427
attah now	4	6258
Gowy gentiles	8	1471
qarab midst	8	7130
Rab many	8	7227
ary lion	8	738
bayn among	8	996
bahamah beasts	8	929
yaar forest	8	3293
kaphyr young	8	3715
adar flocks	8	5739
Tsaown	8	6629
Asar who	8	834
am if	8	518
abar go through	8	5674
shanaym both	8	8147
ramac readeth down	8	7429
Taraph treadeth in pieces	8	2963
yakal can	8	3201
Natsal deliver	8	5337
yad hand	9	3027
Nasa lifted up	9	5375
Tsar adversaries	9	6862
kol all	9	3605
ayab enemies	9	341
karath cut off	9	3772
hayach come to pass	10	1961
yowm day	10	3117
Naam saith	10	5002
cuwc horses	10	5483
al out	10	5921
qarab midst	10	7130
abad destroy	10	6
Markabah chariot	10	4818
karath cut off	11	3772
ayar cities	11	5892
arats land	11	776
harac throw down	11	2040
kol all	11	3605
Mabtsar strong holds	11	4013
kashaph witchcrafts	12	3785
yad hand	12	3027
hayach have	12	1961
lah no	12	3808
owd more	12	5750
anan soothsayers	12	6049
pacyl graven images	13	6456
gam also	13	1571
Matstsabah standing images	13	4676

shaaryth remnant	8	7611
bayn among	8	996
Maasah work	13	4639
yad hands	13	3027
Nathash pluck up	14	5428
asharah groves	14	842
shamad destroy	14	8045
asah execute	15	6213
Naqam vengeance	15	5359
aph anger	15	639
chamah fury	15	2534
Gowy heathen	15	1471
Asar such	15	834
hayach have	15	1961
shama heard	15	8085

ending ch 5

qarab midst	13	7130
shachah worship	13	7812

chapter 6

Na now	1	4994	any myself	6	589
Asar what	1	834	qadam before	6	6924
amar saith	1	559	bamah high	6	1116
quwm arise	1	6965	Alasham God	6	430
ryb contend	1	7378	owlah burnt	6	5930
ath before	1	854	Manchah offerings	6	4503
yanach let	1	3240	agal calves	6	5695
gabah hills	1	1389	shanah year	6	8141
qowl voice	1	6963	ban old	6	1121
ryb controversy	2	7379	Yachuwshauh Lord	+	3068
aythan strong	2	386	ahy will	7	165
arats earth	2	776	ratsan be pleased	7	752?
hayach hath	2	1961	alaph thousands	7	505
yakach plead	2	3198	ayl rams	7	352
Mah what	3	4100	rababah ten thousands	7	7233
hayach have	3	1961	Nachal rivers	7	5158
asah done	3	6213	shaman oil	7	8081
Mah wherein	3	4100	Nathan give up	7	5414
hayach have	3	1961	any my	7	589
ahy I	3	165	bakar firstborn	7	1060
laah wearied	3	3811	pasha transgression	7	6588
anah testify	3	6030	pary fruit	7	6529
alah brought up	4	5927	batan body	7	990
padah redeemed	4	6299	chattah sin	7	2403
bayth house	4	1004	Naphash soul	7	5315
abad servant	4	5650	hayach hath	8	1951
shalach sent	4	7971	Nagad shewed	8	5046
panym before	4	6440	adam man	8	120
Mashach Moses	4	4872	Mah what	8	4100
Aharown Aaron	4	175	Towb good	8	2896
Maryam miriam	4	4813	asah doth	8	6213
ahy my	5	589	darash require	8	1875
zakar remember	5	2142	Mashpat Justly	8	4941
Na now	5	4994	ahabah love	8	160
yaats consulted	5	3289	chacad mercy	8	2617
anah answered	5	6030	yalak walk	8	3212
yakol may	5	3201	Tsana humbly	8	6300
yada know	5	3045	Alasham God	8	430
Tsadaqah righteousness	5	6666	qowl voice	9	6963
Mah wherewith	6	4100	qara crieth	9	7121
qadam come	6	6924	ayar city	9	5892

qadam before	6	6924	adam man	9	120
kaphaph bow	6	3721	Tuwshyah wisdom	9	8454
raah see	9	7200	zara sow	15	2232
Mattah rod	9	4294	qatsar reap	15	7114
my who	9	4310	darak tread	15	1869
hayach hath	9	1961	zayth olives	15	2132
yaad appointed	9	3259	cuwk anoint	15	5480
sham there	10	8033	shaman oil	15	8081
owd yet	10	5750	Tyrowsh sweet	15	8492
owtsar treasures	10	214	yayn wine	15	3196
rasha wickedness	10	7562	shathah drink	15	8354
bayth house	10	1004	yayn wine	15	3196
rasha wicked	10	7563	chuqqah statutes	16	2708
razown scant	10	7332	amar omri	16	6018
ayphah measure	10	374	shamar kept	16	8104
zaam abominable	10	2194	kol all	16	3605
hayach count	11	1961	Maasah works	16	4639
zakah pure	11	2135	bayth house	16	1004
rasha wicked	11	7562	yalak walk	16	3212
Mazan balanes	11	3976	Mowatsah counsels	16	4156
kyc bag	11	3599	Nathan make	16	5414
Marmah deceitful	11	4820	shammah desolation	16	8047
aban weights	11	68	yashab inhabitants	16	3427
ashyr rich	12	6223	kan ha, there of	16	3651
adam men	12	120	sharaqah hissing	16	8322
Mala full	12	4390	kan therefore	16	3651
chamac violence	12	2555	Nasa bear	16	5375
yashab inhabitants	12	3427	charpah reporoach	16	2781
hayach have	12	1961			
dabar spoken	12	1696			
shaqar lies	12	8267			
lashown tongue	12	3956	ending ch 6		
ramyach deceitful	12	7423			
pah mouth	13	6310			
kan therefore	13	3651			
gam also	13	1571			
shuwm make	13	7760			
chalah sick	13	2470			
Nakah smiting	13	5221			
karath making	13	3772			
shamam desolate	13	8074			
al because	13	5921			
chattah sins	13	2403			
attah thou	14	6258			
akal eat	14	398			
shabaa satisfied	14	7646			
yashach casting down	14	3445			
qarab midst	14	7130			
Nacag take hold	14	5253			

palat deliverest, deliver 14 5414
charab sword 14 2719

chapter 7

alalaly woe	1	480	shaphat Judge	3	8199
Naphash M	1	5315	shaal asketh	3	7592
Ahayach I am	1	1961	shalluwn reward	3	7966
ky when	1	3588	gadowl great	3	1419
hayach have	1	1961	kash man	3	376
acaph gather	1	622	dabar uttereth	3	1696
qayts summer	1	7019	havvah mischievous	3	1942
pary fruit	1	6529	Naphash desire	3	5315
alalah grapagleanings	1	5955	kan so	3	3651
batsar vintage	1	1210	abath wrap up	3	5686
sham there	1	8033	Towb best	4	2896
ashkowl cluster	1	811	chadaq brier	4	2312
akal eat	1	398	Tamruer most bitterness	4	8563
Naphash soul	1	5315	yashar upright	4	3477
avah desired	1	183	chadad sharper	4	2300
bakkuerah firstripe	1	1063	Macuwkah thorn hedge	4	4534
pary fruit	1	6529	yowm day	4	3117
chacyd good	2	2623	Tsaphah watch men	4	6822
adam man	2	120	bow cometh	4	835
abad perished	2	6	attah now	4	6258
al out	2	5921	Mabuwkah perplexity	4	3998
arats earth	2	776	aman trust	5	539
sham there	2	8033	raqach friend	5	7543
ayn none	2	369	shuwm put	5	7760
yashar upright	2	3477	batach confidence	5	982
bayn among	2	996	alluph guide	5	441
adam men	2	120	shamar keep	5	3104
kol all	2	3605	pathach doors	5	6607
kazab lie	2	3576	pah mouth	5	6310
arab wait	2	693	shakab lieth	5	7901
dam blood	2	1818	chayq bosom	5	2436
Tsuwd hunt	2	6679	Nabal dishonoureth	6	5034
kash every	2	376	ab father	6	1
kash man	2	376	bath daughter	6	1323
ach brother	2	251	quwm riseth up	6	6965
charam net (zech14:11)	2	2764	Naphash her	6	5315
yakol may	3	3201	am mother	6	517
asah do	3	6213	bath daughter	6	1323
ra evil	3	7451	kallah law	6	3618
shanaym both	3	8147	chamowth mother in law	6	2545
kaph hands	3	3709	kash man's	6	376

yatsab earnestly	3	3190	ayab enemies	6	341
shar prince	3	8269	chanash men	6	582
shaal asketh	3	7592	ratsown own	6	7522
kan therefore	7	3651	bow come	12	935
Tsaphah look	7	6822	gam even	12	1571
arab wait	7	693	Matsowr fortified	12	4692
yasuwa salvation	7	3468	ayar cities	12	5892
any me	7	589	Matsoer fortress	12	4693
shamach rejoice	8	8056	gam even	12	1571
al against	8	5921	Nahar river	12	5104
ayab enemy	8	341	yam sea	12	3220
ky when	8	3588	raq notwithstanding	13	7535
Naphal fall	8	5307	arats land	13	776
quwm arise	8	6965	shamamah desolate	13	8077
yashab sit	8	3427	al because	13	5921
chashak darkness	8	2822	yashab dwell	13	3427
owr light	8	216	Malow therein	13	4393
any me	8	589	pary fruit	13	6529
Nasa bear	9	5375	Maalal doings	13	4611
zaaph indignation	9	2197	raah feed	14	7462
ky because	9	3588	shabat rod	14	7626
hayach have	9	1961	Tsaon flock	14	6629
chata sinned	9	2398	attah thine	14	859
Naphash him	9	5315	Nachalah heritage	14	5159
ad until	9	5704	Asar ahich	14	834
ryb plead	9	7378	shakan dwell	14	7931
any my	9	589	badad solitarily	14	910
ryb cause	9	7379	yaar wood	14	3293
asah execute	9	6213	tavah midst	14	8432
Mashpat Judgment	9	4941	karmal carmel	14	3760
huw he	9	1931	yanach let	14	3240
ahy will	9	165	raah feed	14	7462
yatsa bring forth	9	3318	yowm days	14	3117
any me	9	589	owlam old	14	5769
al to	9	5921	al according	15	5921
owr light	9	216	yatsa coming out	15	3318
raah behold	9	7200	Matsaraym Egypt	15	4714
Tsadaqah righteousness	9	6666	ahy will I	15	165
az then	10	227	raah shew	15	7200
any mine	10	589	pala marvellous	15	6381
ayab enemy	10	341	Mallah things	15	4606
raah see	10	7200	Gowy nations	16	1471
yash it	10	3426	raah see	16	7200
buwshah shame	10	955	chaphar confounded	16	2659
kacah cover	10	3680	kol all	16	3605
Asar which	10	834	gabuwrah might	16	1369
amar said	10	559	shuwm lay	16	7760
any me	10	589	yad hand	16	3027
ayach where	10	346	pah mouth	16	6310

ayn eyes	10	5869
raah behold	10	7200
attah now	10	6253
Marmac trodden down	10	4823
tyt mire	10	2916
chuwts street	10	2351
yowm day	11	3117
gadar walls	11	1447
banah be built	11	1129
chaq decree	11	2706

azan ears	16	241
charash deaf	16	2790
lachak lick up	17	3897
aphar dust	17	6083
chashab like	17	2803
Nakash serpent	17	5175
ragaz move out	17	7264
Macgarath holes	17	4526
chashab like	17	2803
zachal worms	17	2119
arats earth	17	776
pachad afraid	17	6342
yara fear	17	3372
al because	17	5921
my who	18	4310
Al God	18	430
kamow like	18	3644
Nasa pardoneth	18	5375
avon iniquity	18	5771
abar passeth by	18	5674
pasha transgression	18	6588
shaaryth remnant	18	7611
Nachalah heritage	18	5159
chazaq retaineth	18	2388
aph anger	18	639
ad for ever	18	5703
ky because	18	3588
chaphats delighteth	18	2654
chacad mercy	18	2617
huw he	19	1931
ahy will	19	165
shuwb turn again	19	7725
hayach have	19	1961
racham compassion	19	7355
kabash subdue	19	3533
avon iniquities	19	5771
yash thou wilt	19	3426
shalak cast	19	7993
kol all	19	3605
chattaah sins	19	2403
Matsowlah depths	19	4688
yam sea	19	3220
yash thou wilt	20	3426
Nathan perform	20	5414
amath truth	20	571
yaaqob Jacob	20	3290
chacad mercy	20	2617
Asar which	20	834
yash thou hast	20	3426

shaba sworn	20	7650
ab fathers	20	1
yowm days	20	3117
qadamah old	20	6924

ending ch 7